Children of the World

My Life in
INDIA

Alex Woolf

Cavendish Square

New York

Published in 2015 by Cavendish Square Publishing, LLC
243 5th Avenue, Suite 136, New York, NY 10016

First Edition

Website: cavendishsq.com

This publication represents the opinions and views of the author based on his or her personal experience, knowledge, and research. The information in this book serves as a general guide only. The author and publisher have used their best efforts in preparing this book and disclaim liability rising directly or indirectly from the use and application of this book.

CPSIA Compliance Information: Batch #WW15CSQ

All websites were available and accurate when this book was sent to press.

Library of Congress Cataloging-in-Publication Data
Woolf, Alex, 1964-
 My life in India / Alex Woolf.
    pages cm — (Children of the world)
 Includes index.
 ISBN 978-1-50260-048-6 (hardcover) ISBN 978-1-50260-049-3 (paperback)
 ISBN 978-1-50260-277-0 (ebook)
 1. India—Social life and customs—Juvenile literature. 2. Children—India—Juvenile literature. I. Title.

 DS421.W743 2015
 954—dc23

 2014026346

Editor: Joe Harris
Designer: Ian Winton

All photography courtesy of Money Sharma / Demotix / Corbis

Printed in the United States of America

Contents

Morning

Hi! I'm Rajiv. I am twelve years old and I live with my mother, father, and sister here in Delhi, India.

> **Rajiv says ...**
> Go away, Mom. It's too early. I want to sleep!

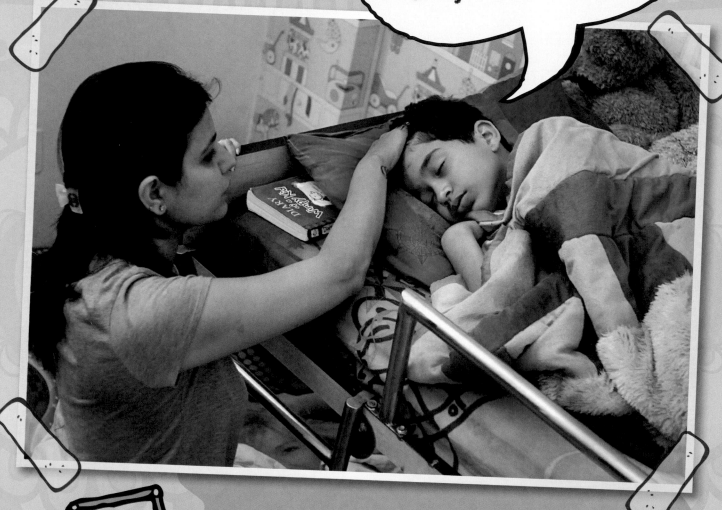

I get up at 6:30. After my shower, I get dressed. School uniforms are **compulsory** in India.

Our school has a typical Indian school uniform: long, dark blue trousers, a light-colored shirt, and a dark tie.

As I tie my laces on my shoes, I hear Mom calling me for breakfast.

My Country

India is an enormous country of 1.2 billion people, located in South Asia. It has a warm climate. Delhi is in northern India.

Getting Ready

Mom makes us breakfast. This morning she makes us an omelette and chai, which is a spiced tea from India.

Rajiv says ...

I eat breakfast with my sister, Diya.

Diya is nine and we go to the same school. We live in a modern apartment in Vasant Kunj, in southwest Delhi. My parents are partners in their own business. They work from home.

I brush my hair
and make myself
look good for school.

Mom and Dad
wave goodbye
as Diya and
I set off for
school.

Indian Breakfasts

We eat a very light breakfast. Traditional
breakfasts in northern India could include
a **paratha** (pa-RAWT-ah) or *chapati*
(sha-PA-tee) (types of flatbread) served
with vegetable curry, curd, and pickles.

 **7:30 AM**

Going to School

Diya and I attend Ryan International School, which is also in Vasant Kunj. Diya is in Class IV and I am in Class VII.

Rajiv says... We take the bus to school each morning.

 Our school has over forty buses carrying children to and from different parts of the city each day. We must always be polite and listen to the driver.

8

On the bus I chat with my friend Arjun.

It takes us twenty minutes to get to school. I have my cricket bat with me. Cricket is my passion.

Delhi

Delhi, where I live, is India's biggest city, with a population of twenty-two million people. It contains the city of New Delhi, India's capital.

9

School Assembly

There are many Ryan International Schools in India. They are private schools, so we must pay to be educated here. Most Indian children go to government schools, which are free.

Rajiv says ...

We always start assembly with a prayer.

We are lucky because we go to a modern, well-equipped school. We have a library, computers, and excellent **facilities** for sports, art, and music.

We listen carefully to a speech from the principal.

Today, I get a chance to address the whole school. I enjoy public speaking. Of course, I talk about my favorite subject: cricket!

Indian Schools

Most children in India attend school. In poorer areas of cities, or in remote areas, there can be up to sixty people in a classroom, and they have very few books.

Lessons

Lessons begin at 8:30. There are thirty students in my class. At our school, everyone speaks English.

Rajiv says ...

Today we are learning about the human body.

Our lessons include English, math, **Hindi**, science, geography, history, and art.

My friend Arnav and I have made a model to show how teeth are arranged in our mouths.

I am learning computer science. We are lucky to have computers – 78 percent of Indian schools don't have one.

Languages of India

There are over 1,600 languages spoken in India today, and eighteen official languages. The most widely spoken language is Hindi, but English is also very common.

Art and Music

At ten o'clock, some of us go to the music room, where we are learning to play instruments. I am learning the drums.

Rajiv says ...

I am learning to play rock and pop rhythms.

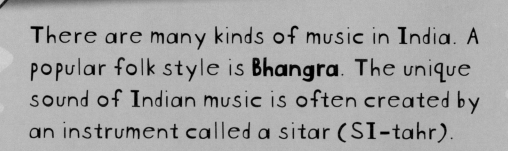

There are many kinds of music in India. A popular folk style is **Bhangra**. The unique sound of Indian music is often created by an instrument called a sitar (SI-tahr).

We're preparing for a concert at the end of term, which is in June. In India, the school year begins in April and ends in March. We have vacations in June and December.

In our art class, we're making mosaics out of colored pieces of paper.

Art of India

Our country is famous for its art. Indian artists through the ages have made magnificent bronze sculptures, murals (wall paintings), miniature paintings, and jewelry.

Sport

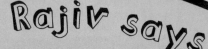

During breaktime, I eat my snack. Mom made me a *paratha* with *dal* (DAHL) (lentil stew) and *raita* (RI-ee-tah) (yogurt sauce).

Rajiv says ...
I chat with my friends about cricket. I'm happy because India is winning in its test match against England.

Cricket is the most popular sport in India. In any open space, you will often find kids playing it. Our national team has won the Cricket World Cup twice!

16

I enjoy physical education classes, but sometimes I find it hard to keep in time with everyone else.

I am the opening batsman for my local team. Here I am practicing in the nets.

Indian Sport

Other popular sports in India include field hockey, football (soccer), badminton, basketball, and *kabaddi* (KA-bah-dee), a type of wrestling.

Hometime

2:00 PM

At two o'clock, the bell rings. It's time to go home. Most children take the school bus. A few walk or are picked up by their parents.

Rajiv says ...
Before we leave school we always say our prayers.

Our school follows the Christian faith, but it is open to children of all religions. The majority of schools here are Christian.

Around 82 percent of people in India are Hindu. But many other religions are also practiced, including **Islam**, Christianity, **Sikhism, Buddhism,** and **Jainism**.

I chat with Aseem on the school bus. He is a Sikh.

Hinduism

Hinduism is one of the oldest religions in the world. It developed around 5,000 years ago. It is a colorful religion with many rituals. Hindus believe in lots of gods and goddesses.

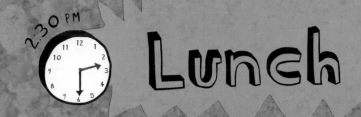

Lunch

2:30 PM

The bus reaches my stop at about two-thirty. My mother is there waiting for me. Our apartment is just a few minutes' walk from here.

Many people in India are vegetarian, meaning they don't eat meat. Hindus believe that the cow is a sacred animal and they never eat beef.

Rajiv says...

I'm starving, Mom! Is lunch ready?

We eat our food on plates, but traditionally Indian food is served on a *thali (TAH-Lee)*, a large, metal platter, with helpings of different dishes served in small metal bowls.

While we eat, Mom asks us about our day.

Indian Spices

Spices are essential to Indian cooking, giving flavor to even the simplest dishes. Important spices include cumin, coriander, turmeric, fenugreek, ginger, mustard seed, and cardomom.

Out and About

The weather is warm and sunny in the afternoon, and we go out and enjoy ourselves. I practice cricket with my dad.

Our winter lasts from November to February, and our summer from April to June. The monsoon (rainy) season lasts from June to October.

Rajiv says ...

Dad bowls some balls to me in our garage.

Grandpa visits, and he takes us out for a walk.

We stop at a **street vendor** and Grandpa buys us each an ice cream.

Indian Street Games

We like to play *chupan chupai* (hide and seek), chain (an "it" game, where those who are caught join hands to form a lengthening chain) and *kancha* (a game using marbles).

Shopping

Later in the afternoon, Mom takes us shopping. Diya wants some crayons and I need a new cricket ball.

Rajiv says ...

Thank you, Mom. This is perfect!

I like the look of this bat, too. But Mom says no. Diya is getting impatient for her crayons.

24

Delhi is a huge international city, and you can buy almost anything here. As well as general stores like this one, there are street markets, shopping malls, arcades, and expensive **boutiques**.

Diya gets her crayons, and Mom buys herself a tube of badminton shuttlecocks.

Indian Money

The official **currency** of India is the rupee, which is divided into **100** *paise*. Rupee comes from the **Sanskrit** word rupyakam (roo-pee-AH-kam), meaning silver coin.

At Home

When we get home from the shops, we do our homework and then play a board game. We watch TV while Mom prepares our supper.

Rajiv says ...

Mom helps me with my English homework.

After we've finished our homework, we play a board game with Dad. The game is called Parcheesi (similar to Ludo) and it's very popular in India.

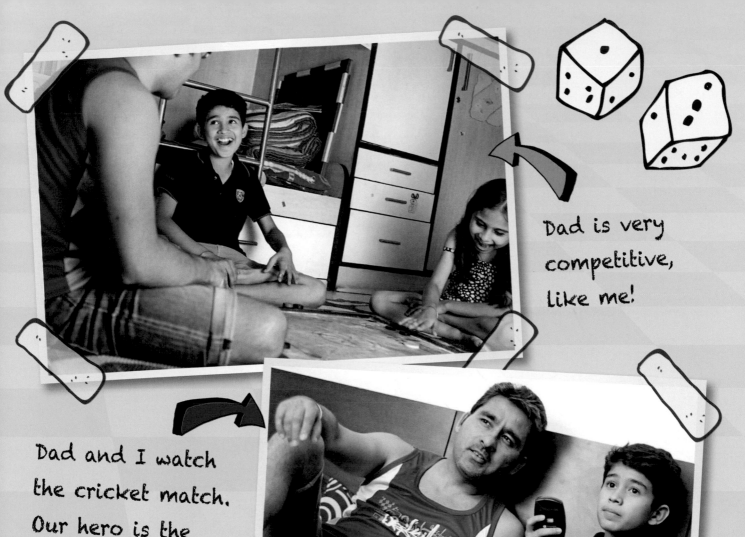

Dad is very competitive, like me!

Dad and I watch the cricket match. Our hero is the batsman Gautam Gambhir, who was born in Delhi.

Indian Pastimes

In their spare time, Indians like watching movies (we have a huge film industry based in Mumbai). We play games like Parcheesi, chess, and backgammon. Some people enjoy classical dance or **yoga**. Kite flying is also very popular.

Evening Meal

7:30 PM

At half past seven, we sit down for supper. Mom has made us chicken and vegetable curries with chapatis, **palak paneer** (PAH-lehk pah-NEER), dal, chopped onion, and chutney.

> **Rajiv says...**
> We don't eat with silverware but use the chapati to scoop up our food.

Indian food varies from region to region. Northern India is known for *tandoori* cooking. Meat is **marinaded** in yogurt and spices before being cooked in a *tandoor (tahn-DUHR)* (clay oven).

Bread is popular in northern India, because the land isn't very good for growing rice. *Chapati* is a round flatbread, cooked on a *tava* (TAH-vah) (hotplate). *Nan*, a puffy bread made with yeast, is cooked in a tandoor.

Diya falls asleep quickly, but I'm not very tired so I think I'll read for a while. Goodnight!

Indian Sweets

West Bengal in northeast India is famous for its sweets, especially *rasgullas* and *sandesh*. *Rasgullas* (res-goo-LAHS) are small, spongy balls of curd cheese and sugar. *Sandesh* (sahn-DAYSH) are similar but flavored with ingredients like coconut and rose water.

Glossary

Bhangra A popular music combining Indian folk traditions with Western pop music.

boutiques Small stores selling fashionable clothes or accessories.

Buddhism A religion founded in northeastern India in the fifth century BCE.

compulsory Required by law or by a rule.

currency The money used in a particular country.

facilities Space or equipment for doing something.

Hindi An official language of India, and the most widely spoken language of northern India.

Hinduism The major religion of India, Bangladesh, Sri Lanka, and Nepal. Hindus worship a large number of gods and goddesses.

Islam The religion of Muslims, founded in the seventh century CE by the Prophet Muhammad.

Jainism A religion founded in India in the sixth century BCE by the Jina Vardhamana Mahavira.

marinaded (of meat, fish, or other food) Soaked in a sauce before cooking to flavor or soften it.

palak paneer A dish consisting of pureed spinach and paneer (farmer's cheese).

paratha An unleavened (made without yeast) flatbread (slightly thicker than a chapati) made with wholewheat flour.

Sanskrit An ancient language of India and the root of many northern Indian languages.

Sikhism A religion founded in Punjab (a region in northwestern India) in the fifteenth century CE by Guru Nanak.

street vendor Someone who sells things in the street, either from a stall or van or with their goods laid out on the pavement.

yoga A Hindu form of exercise and meditation (deep thinking) for health and relaxation.

Further Information

Websites

www.bbc.co.uk/news/world-south-asia-12557384
A profile of India from the BBC.

www.facts-about-india.com
A large site containing information about India, its geography, climate, culture, sports, and other things.

www.historyforkids.org/learn/india/food
A website all about Indian food.

www.theschoolrun.com/homework-help/india
Interesting facts, a photo gallery, a list of famous Indians, and a quiz.

www.timeforkids.com/destination/india
Facts about India, including a sightseeing guide, history timeline, Hindi phrases, and a day in the life of a typical Indian child.

travel.nationalgeographic.com/travel/countries/india-facts/
A guide to India, including fast facts, map, photos, and video.

Further Reading

Bingham, Jane. *India.* My Holiday In. London, England: Wayland, 2014.

Brooks, Susie. *India.* Unpacked! London, England: Wayland, 2014.

Humble, Darryl. *India.* Countries in Our World. London, England: Franklin Watts, 2013.

Powell, Jillian. *India.* My Country. London, England: Franklin Watts, 2013.

Savery, Annabel. *India.* Been There. London, England: Franklin Watts, 2014.

Index